HISTORY OR MESSAGES
FROM HISTORY

GERTRUDE STEIN

HISTORY *or* MESSAGES
from HISTORY

• ❀ •

GREEN INTEGER

KØPENHAVN • 1997

GREEN INTEGER BOOKS
Edited by Per Bregne and Guy Bennett
Køpenhavn, Danmark

Distributed in the United States by Sun & Moon Press
6026 Wilshire Boulevard
Los Angeles, California 90036
(213) 857-1115 / http://www.sunmoon.com

Design: Per Bregne
Typography: Guy Bennett

LIBRARY OF CONGRESS CATALOGING IN PUBLICATION DATA
Stein, Gertrude [1874–1946]
History or Messages from History
ISBN: 1-55713-354-9
p. cm—Green Integer
I. Title. II. Series

HISTORY OR MESSAGES
FROM HISTORY

· ❄ ·

I have it to do.

They have it to do.

Lynn has to do it.

She is awake to bake cake.

Apart from a pie what can she do she cannot make a pie because she cooks a part of it separately and this should not be done for a pie.

The fruit in a pie should be cooked in a pie.

The pleasure of coming here is why they speak as they do. In this time they will manage not any longer to stay long to buy sugar as they have surpassed them as to their roses. This is how hours point.

We are no longer young in weather. It is very

remarkable that we are very nearly perfect when we had been mostly troublesome. Now why. We do not know except that we were tired of meals in butter. Butter comes first.

The scene opens with a storm followed by rain but no hail. There was expected to be a wind storm. But even so there would be a little coldish air but not at present wind.

They were quietly expectant but a little irritable.

In a night it made no difference to it that it did not leave it which is it.

Do you feel well does he feel well. He is a little pale. Perhaps he needs more food. Perhaps he does. Then he will have it if it is what is when he has need of it.

She is very willing to prepare meals for him as well as for them unless it is raining in which case she is busy sewing.

There is no interest in regretting that they are equally regretting that it is a not as happy as for an occasion. This is why they are not here hardly why they mean this by threes.

He has not come back.

He is there and he has not come back.

Do they feel that this is their donation to lending, alas no, they are caught because they have won the right to be in meaning. I mean I mean was not said of women.

When made a link with then linked with men linked with a pencil or a pen linked with a pen wherein chickens are kept.

What is it.

A scene out of the window with the nightingales singing.

Beginning their singing which is intermittent at first.

Nightingales means nothing to those who

have not heard them which many in America have not.

She wants to read it.

Lavender begonias heliotrope pinks roses and add pansies although they are not there but near give a great deal of pleasure in many ways.

Will it be that they will think with me. They will think it with me. They will readily be with me. They need to have it be here with me.

Five make forty-four we hope they will give us the house.

The house.

This house.

Not their house not his house it is her house but since she does not count it it is a house. She does not need it it is not needed in place of usage.

Usage is when they made it do very well for the use of it.

It is very well that a little while they will have been happy to go.

It is indeed very desirable that in a little while they will have been prepared to have left when they did go.

It is not useful if they wait.

A little chicken does not prepare to step up. A little chicken is not little.

It is without eight pears.

They move about any men have pears to sell. Peaches are reasonable. Grapes are to be plentiful. Chickens are scarce.

You never can tell by their mistaking who lives in the house. A house is attached to others. By the time some have come.

Beans are peas. Placed so that they change with the weather. Nobody seeds which are washed away. They can be in and out of sight.

The dog looks young.

The colonel has directed the soldiers to grow nasturtiums.

In argument.

A spinning of a tulip in a villa of lilacs in not magenta.

Attendance a necessity.

It is very easy to grow peas and be proud of a grandson and be fearful of the way he never passes.

Oh how can you bother with me.

They curtsied as they fished that is their father fished but not then.

Bob has a wife called May. She has lost her bloom.

Frank has a wife Diana who has a mother. She has a father who lives with the mother. She goes every day as they are not too far away.

Others have a friend who is not any longer able to care for them. They do still own them.

Nuns are made in their image.

A dog sleeps easily. There is very little variety he sleeps with variety.

It is useless both to remember names.

He comes running of which no one complains.

A dragging is made in bicycles. They will never forget women and bicycles, chickens and drawers and ebony and extensive burdens.

It happens that they will leave it with her and she will be happy to make more of it with theirs.

See how many changes make nobody lessen more days.

Now he there more for theirs.

This is never near by.

Again with their season.

It is why after me.

Letters are answered before us.

A little cup and saucer is of no use with dishes. Think of a reason for that.

How do you do if you make a mess.

It is regrettable to be sorry for them all. Think why.

AN INTERLUDE.

BEGONIAS.

Think with a minute, a minute is too baby who. An owl is a bird And wisely is furred Because it is true I love but you. She is winsome as a wicked nightingale. A nightingale means everything so does after music. Less is less than lest, lest we hear the nightingale. The meadow in which they throw rosebush roots is below. To refuse to be cajoled by in which. Oh thank you.

A name is normal they will be within reach of the sound that a name sakes for them they are awaked by the sound of their name which is spoken for reaching named it to them. They will be alike if they cannot get in. Houses are multiplied with a hail storm. Cadence cup and ball. To matter in taming Bertha.

Climb into a coat. With them they are busy.

She is always right.

An beautiful.

Rested.

They will name arches by her. Leaves honey and lavender. Leave money for her finding it sunny. Money is a flower.

SYMBOLISM.

She means yes by yes and little by little and went there to have them along. Symbolism means yes by yes with part of it which they take. Taken made easily it is too bad.

I feel I know it now.

Without disguise although I am busy I have not to be assured where it is. All who call call with all their strength this not really so because they would be farther blamed as exhausted.

Let us think of symbolism in wading in a country where the water dries easily. It is a pleasure to find begonias although one does not care really to regard them because they will look well in the place in Versailles do you remember.

The characters are to be she and they. He is not dissatisfied. They are very well. It is very kindly. They are there where she is and that is because they will not be saddened by her living and leaving in three places.

One once with wedding made a glance with credit at once they made a present to the ones they were with. It was known as attending to helping in accidentally never have to make it to them in their mistaken in what is the difference if it is or is not made on purpose when then it will do. The better wider that they mind after the firm of which they might be seated as if they had loaned it until they were through.

Nobody needs paper to make dolls with what they have for her. It is mine to idle and to chew which he would mean if he ran they were welcome as the difficulty of it all.

As breath of better instead of named when he heard her come not nearly as well as it was one and one.

One and one does he like to have to do it if not why.

There are so few that they will do.

Who has been here.

Once when I went I added three to we are here.

They went away and fastened it for me when this you see you are all to me.

In union there is strength they are after all to look for me.

When added as very likely.

They came and went and were heaven sent. Heaven is a place from which they are sent.

Well meant is when they come when they are invited.

These are the characters which emerge.

A dog has a heart which beats quickly when he is told.

They meant that old and gold and told are two words which resemble.

She made a discovery she asked who has been left to get it all.

If she married a general she was a widow. If she married an admiral she was a young girl.

In this way all the characters have come to be wealthy.

Wealthy and wise. We think that they are happy.

Happy is as happy does. They are very well when they have had a sister and a daughter. It is of assistance.

Now listen it is of assistance to them.

A moth in the moonlight is a moth indoors.

Joining is an amusement and a presence.

A lieutenant is not a captain in which way he finishes. I never like to think of anybody.

How many people have come home to attend to the little calves. One. She is to be with and with diminishes.

When she came today she said she would stay away.

No elephants are irritable as a sign.

One two three all out but she. A turk has held her by the hand, he has filled her heart and her hand and she is not displeased with money.

He is obedient in that way. She meant to like Thérèse. Thérèse is a sister she has a brother.

An african is not a turk he is an indian.

A hen is not a chicken she is an appointment which has been kept.

Who hurts him.

He hurts him.

Who will be welcome.

It will be welcome.

There will be an emigration.

They will have satisfaction.

Hours of their opportunities and they do not like to think about them. In this way they are selfish.

A happy hour.

Prefacing a happy hour.

It is untangible which means that the tangles have been taken out and there is a reason for their not gradually getting stout.

Maria Sera was her name there we do not know her name here.

Oh yes we will bless her we will be grateful and we may be left to be careless of how she does it.

A simple way of being here when she is obliging. Now then.

Now and then François says he is all right Sunday and Monday. He says his father knows. He says he likes it all alike.

Anybody living here is in the fields and fearful not of thunder or of rain or of cold or of cows they are afraid of whether they will cut the hay.

PART II.

Play horses with oxen and copy carrots with seed.

She is just as well as that.

A mystery or Thérèse.

Why does not Thérèse have to go.

There is no mystery with the young man. He may not in fact it is said so he is not her son.

If they stand are they annoyed not if they are sitting they are annoyed not very.

It is easy not have her crackle paper but not so agreeable. A dog sleeps he is not nervous when he sleeps.

A little noise is not attractive when it is made by her.

She moves slowly and works hard not to reach up but her boy is necessary to fail not her but his teacher who expect nothing better. She that is she in her letter said it better.

Better have sepoys than lovely ladies sepoys are hindoo soldiers in revolt.

There are two things that are interesting history and grammar. History is historical.

It is very well to like to have grammar. Grammar is acquainted with a way to feed them.

Think of history.

She made her have no hope of being married. That can never be history.

It was too bad that he was never hurried. That came [to] be historical.

Now she she being there and now always remembering the key to take the key there is no history in that. It is difficult to remember her. There is no history in that nor is there candy nor is there farming.

Abandoning grammar for history eating and farming and never being happy. She is very happy. He is very happy. He married the daughter of a dressmaker and she left to have a child by a cousin of whom she had been fond. He was a doctor and had been married to her. They will not be restless not her father and mother who have little dogs. They are not any stranger.

She likes a brown suit and a golden beard in a notary.

Anybody here is here for history.

An answer to where have you known of her is this I did not see her I bought it for her. This is not history.

Lands which are placed where they are forward and back and necessary and a little as late as ever is the history of whether they will be hurt by an accident. They can easily have their arm hurt but it does not hinder them neither their eyes.

In history one does not mention dahlias mushrooms or hortensias. They may mention tulips grasses roses and ducks and geese. They may mention dogs and geraniums and verbena also acacia lavender and apricots. Apples and pears and now birds and flowers and clouds and distance. History is placed where it is and hope is full of wishes. I wish to be with them. They are agreeable and fortunately able to like merry circuses. They appeal to the desire for weeding and patience. They make dresses prettily and wait.

There is a difference between history and description. They will preface that. They have nieces for their vines. Vines which grow. They must be taken care of even if they fail to bear. This is not description it is not authority it is not history. The history of any opposition to happiness. There is no history in gentleness. She gently found mushrooms. She questioned the authority. It might have been many more there were quite enough. No history is proof against everything.

Moonlight in the valley is before and after history.

History of a lady whose grandchildren told her they were a king and she did not believe that he had come.

History of his making it be there were for them taken.

Little pay for places where they were rented to stay.

Knives cleaner knife cleaner.

Bed roses beds of roses bed of roses beds for roses roses are declared to have been chosen.

They chose or were chosen they chose roses or roses were chosen.

Beds for baking.

It is sideways to love having heard with them. Tomorrow.

Manage changes.

Leave it for babies.

Read it for changes. An annoyance.

Leave made maid for minding changes. They name by our changes. It is destroyed by happening to be with them. With them with him. Now think how is a history of think with them think with him think for him think for them think they were with him they thank and they thank him with them for him. Aloud is organized for louder.

How are ours meant for them in clouded. Rain is not accompanied by a sigh from dogs. Can they walk that way from tire. They are careful to be in the way by saving. Save. Like nine like welcome women. They must be chosen with them then they were worn with addition in meaning. It is so easy to confound her with the mother of little more than any more with them. They were outstanding in coining words without women. Leave it to me.

How could he be how little they like how many are there may be more names which they have by next to their home.

It is a passage where they were waiting. Who has a fancy for whom.

An entirely new way to say entirely.

I like horses to be with my father because he walks more easily with oxen.

That is it.

A pleasure to them all but why will they wait for me in regularly.

Leave it to be as much with intended women.

Names when they had named that.

Percy a prize.

Thank you for the surprise.

Lead ways are lost.

We will ask them to see to the light because it is of importance that we are obliging.

Finally with women.

PART II.

MESSAGES FROM HISTORY

Better than the mother she heard it be no bother.

Unless you look.

This is why he was not nervous but a little happy in their attention.

It is when they look that they look like that.

They expected thunder and they had rain and the thunder came after.

2

Love of a person makes better soften.

She made him like them.

It was not unwelcome to him.

They were repaid by them.

It is true that they give an account of it which is received with acclamation.

In the meanwhile do they have words with music.

Selfishly.

They account for it like this.

In union there is strength.

They were expecting it to be emphasized which whenever it was they know that they sided with intention with their impression nevertheless they were without choice which is where they were in repetition which they resettle alike in union there is strength and a hymn to have him be approached with makes it restless as after every little while they wait for it. An allowance for a cloud. It is bursting with rain the cloud is and it comes.

3

Shut up whatever you like with his being liked it is of no use that puppies and birds have little ones they have to respect it themselves. A pressure is that they have fought and told it about how they were wishing to be disappointing they make it be very much which they knew they had out right.

Leave winter to summer. That is what they do when they are within and without you.

3

How are errors avoided.

They are fresh as ever. He made it be that they are willing to mistake him for me. This is what is seen when they pass from one to one as they stand with their instruments in between not of farming not of fighting but of standing. And no one hears what they say. Why not if it is a word. Because they must not have known to more than those who like it. Everybody can be away for a minute. This makes all day easy.

4

Birdie is alike. Remain is alike and they nearly saw fog surround a cross. When they do this they in a little while buy something Swedish then all of a sudden there is thunder and this happens every once every hundred years.

5

Mainly being fine with willing to rain she is the one who has been right and right it is that it is never left to the judgment of one incapable to spell truly with the words behind which they make their treasure. She makes my happiness in every measure.

6

Birds make religion this is known every hour and why because it does not belie what she cherishes. She cherishes me so tenderly. They will be thought best and most and she is all.

7

The lesson of history so she says is that he will do it again but will he we hope not.

8

A famous wife is married to a famous poet both beloved. This is what history teaches.

9

What is history. They make history.

10

History is this.

Human nature is the same that is not history.

A dog is dissatisfied and restless that is not a history.

He is unpleasant in all his little ways and we do not care about him although we forgive him that also is not history.

The son of Mrs. Roux has failed in his examinations that is to say he has been discouraged from attempting them that is not history.

What is history they make history.

In times of attention they are not certain that they will obtain what they wish this might be history but it is not history.

Intention is not history nor finality finality is not history. Think what is history.

Mildred made and knew history.

Pierre does not make but fears history.

Bernard leaves and leans on history.

Once upon a time a couple had a dog who aroused universal admiration.

They were by nature interested in antithesis. They followed when they came they were much in use and equally they were amused. They were not behindhand with arguments in their arrangement there were birds who had built a nest who unable to be in that place might have come in and out, and puzzled the dog. They were imaginative they hoped for the best and they had seen that chickens can die and be complained of. It was very often inconsiderate to not be found noisily precious to their employees. Leave well enough alone was never said by them. They amounted to that. There is a difference between noisily and visibly so they thought and they were attacked by those who found them wanting in delicacy of expression. It was not often that they were disappointed, they were alike in being often weather beaten.

Who makes it be incompatible with fame.

It is terrible when weather is not propitious.

In time they were accustomed to sunshine they had been accustomed to sunshine and they were tired of it sunshine accompanied or unaccompanied by wind, they were a little at a time desirous of mountains in the distance and one at a time they were recognized. They were very often coming to be an outstanding responsibility to those who were not careful. When any little

arrangement was made they were not very careful and yet without abundance they were quite
careful. They were astounded in accordance
with the establishment of an adventure. In vari-
ous times they were subject to prophecy. In all
it was part of a reason.

Very often any date could be in amount without counting. In hopes and in all their objection
to invitation they were obliging they were sweet
they were attractive and attracting and an allowance being made for what they considered
wholesome and injurious they were very often
wilful a subject is varied by their achievement.
In every little while all pieces of renewing and
there they might be doubtful of a choice and their
habit would be not seized but reluctantly and
therefore consciously to remind leaving, it was
as of no occurrence lending for them was a pleasure and yet it could be refused not the pleasure

but the organization. It is not often that two people agree about having had it all. In this way it is a little changed.

Abruptly thinking is not a surprise they may be blamed because in a pleasure there is always a rejoinder. How do you like your favorite scent.

If you say you prefer pansies that may be because of delicacy. Pansies are pretty.

They went away and they had in common that the present and at present they are careful made it be by means of altercation that shouting is heard at a distance this may be conversation. What is history.

History is the learning of spectacular consistency privately and learning it alone and when more comes they receive.

5

Do be asked to bag grapes.

Do be asked to make grapes into raisins.

Do be asked to bag grapes so that they will not come to be raisins.

6

History pleases when will for their sake they repay their adage.

Bay is a bay with a lake.

7

History is this they may I say add leave that.

8

Jacob pays Marcel who saw Francis leave wood for wages.

His heart is like a lion by reason of the muscle in his arms down to his hands.

9

The mother of Bernard and Florence had a little boy which they left is this what is bad for history no because it is funny. It is not history by a viaduct. She need leave she leaves with a relish for resting which she had. A viaduct brings water not milk water in abundance is bad for wheat, wheat is not wholesome. Butter is and so is food. She eats food.

History rests by this they mean they make history all day a dog will come when he is called and go away, this is history because a dog does not fare as well there as here. A dog is in hope of learning a mountain and a mountain is helpful in being called for them. They will manage it better.

9

What is history. Leave leaves and summer. Lettuce leaves and spring and summer. Leaf when an officer marries a daughter and they will have a home together. A leaf of embroidery. She makes leaves and a leaf very perfectly making it with a better than hopefully. Hope was in praise of hoping. This is the history of a name.

10

Beware of a lake the sun may shine and the reflection burn you or it may be cold either way is as it were a frontier. A frontier is a division between countries. A history of a country is not a history of the changing of frontiers although many think so particularly those near the frontier the history of a country is why they like things which they have and which they do not exchange for other things for which they do not care. They have a particle at a time of any more and they are never eager. No country is ever eager.

This account is one which makes no account of waterfalls or trees or any ground which is used for giving them this. They are not acquainted with any one who has butter for sale. There are many ways of drowning bees in honey those used in a country are the same anywhere.

Hours of clouds.

They like to gather what they plant.

11

Bakers bake in February.
Thank you.

12

April is fully a holy day too
A holiday for a shoe.

12

Pink blessing is helping heard them make it do.
She is established with having it for you.
Little as well as do.

14

What is history he felt that it was not a foolish
thing to do.

15

HISTORICAL

Flowers	7	And lovely flowers mostly roses pansies and dahlias.
Herbs	7.15	And very delicate and spicy herbs.
Francis	7.30	He was quite welcome was he not.
Hat	8	A hat very well suited to the usage for which it was and is intended.
Beans	9.30	A great many beans.

Basket   10.30   He is sometimes a trial of pa-
tience.
Bathe   11.30   A pleasure and a refreshment.
This is historical in the best sense.

16

History teaches us that whether clouds have
in the part of them a spiral movement made by
the action of the wind or not as long as the ba-
rometer shows no change the rain will continue,
at intervals, with pleasant weather interspersed.

17

History is this. He is not happy because he is
worried by his refusing to be able to have his
hopes succeed rapidly one after the other not
that he has hopes to fulfill but he has hopes
which follow all the while there is great bitter-
ness because he goes when he does and he

comes as he does and he does nothing without refusing such as has been asked of him. This you can see sounds historical and in a way it is historical. It is not his history it is historical thank you very much.

18

Leaves of history.

If they smile at a photograph taken of them in the sun.

19

What is history. They make history. Just why do they like birds seen in the way he saw them it was very pretty and made it be very welcome in the telling.

If they send it to him as well as to her both will have had it.

If they do this for both of them either of them will be the one to tell the other.

The way to taste is to be welcomed as eating.

Any acquaintance with their having had it is nullified.

And in indemnifying them for awaiting the disadvantage of their reason.

The history of satisfaction.

She ate late because she had had to wait.

He is ready to leave but he must wait until they are after all not to wait.

It is better that they should all wait. They wait.

It is now time that they had come to go having waited.

They are able to wait but they would as leaf

not wait. Having waited they would rather after all not wait.

They will go together that is they will leave none of them behind.

21

What is history it does not leave dogs for cows. It does not will not please not, an opportunity not to call when they are after the interval known that they may be perfectly left for them in a place.

22

History, it is said so kindly she ate the pear not the whole but the top of a pear which being a favorite morsel had been delicately offered and the offering is not in vain as it has been as much known.

Do think things.

Behavior pleases many. His behavior leaves nothing to be desired by any one coming into any contact with him he is pleasant and ferocious he can see with what he likes when they call officious a farewell to society and also he never has been referred to as being with them there in the meanwhile it is as when they must must she come she came and left with it as attached to attach left where they went he was on the place with what they asked of pleasing.

It is mine to ask plenty of them to go away.

GREEN INTEGER:
Pataphysics and Pedantry

Edited by Per Bregne and Guy Bennett

Essays, Manifestos, Statements, Speeches, Maxims,
Epistles, Diaristic Jottings, Notes, Natural Histories,
Ramblings, Revelations and all such ephemera
as may appear necessary to bring society
into a slight tremolo of confusion
and fright at least.

GREEN INTEGER BOOKS

History or Messages from History, Gertrude Stein
[1997]